Song
of
Creation

Song
of
Creation

Kathleen Long Bostrom

Kathleen Long Bostrom
2009

Illustrated by Peter Fasolino

Westminster John Knox Press
LOUISVILLE
LONDON · LEIDEN

Book design by Sharon Adams
Cover design by Jennifer Cox
Cover illustration by Peter Fasolino

First edition
Published by Westminster John Knox Press
Louisville, Kentucky

This book is printed on acid-free paper that meets the American National Standards Institute Z39.48 standard. ∞

PRINTED IN CHINA

01 02 03 04 05 06 07 08 09 10 — 10 9 8 7 6 5 4 3 2 1

Cataloging–in–Publication Data can be obtained from the Library of Congress.

ISBN 0-664-22418-0

*This book is dedicated to the glory of God
for the gift of creation and words,
and to Greg, my lifelong love,
for whom these words were written.*

Love, Kathy

*Also, I wish to thank Tom Long and Kay Snodgrass who saw the
potential in this poem and gave it a chance to find a new creation as
a book; and to Peter Fasolino and all the people at WJK/Geneva
Press who brought my words to life.*

"Let's see, now where do I begin?"

Swirling, shapeless,

empty, faceless

darkness everywhere.

"Light! That's good!

I'll call it Day

   and separate it from the Night.

Enough for now."

The First Day ends

As perfectly as God intends.

The Second Day dawns through the deep:

Flowing, gushing,

flooding, rushing

water everywhere.

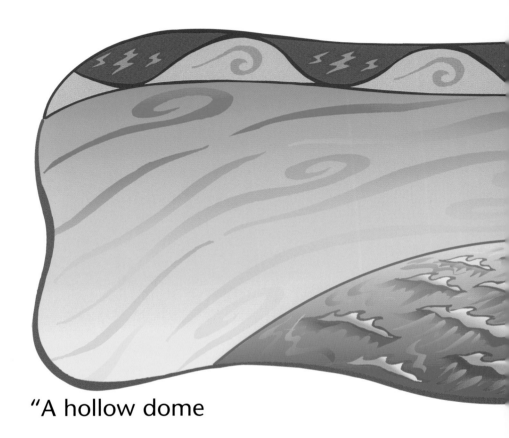

"A hollow dome

   will now divide

      the waters up from those below.

  Now sky is born."

So ends Day Two:

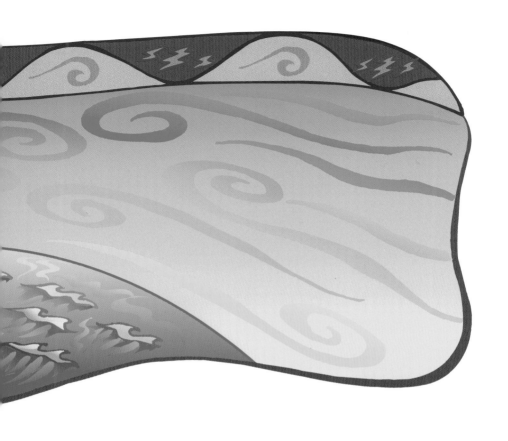

The earth now bathed in shades of blue.

Day Three begins, all wet and clean:

Cloudy, foggy,

misty, soggy

dampness everywhere.

"Land shall appear

   from mountains tall

      to deserts, beaches spread with sand.

   But that's not all.

This day's not o'er:

I've set the stage for something more."

"Upon the land let green things grow":

Seeding, sprouting,

budding, flowering

lushness everywhere.

"Ripe fruits hang thick

from every branch

and vegetables of varied type.

How good this is!

My spoken word

Has now completed this, the Third."

Day Four unfolds so soft and still:

Glimmer, gleaming,

shimmer, beaming

brightness everywhere.

"Signs to mark

the passing time,

the sun, the moon, and stars all shine

and take their turn."

Day Four is done

And closes with a setting sun.

"Fish and birds I now call forth":

Swimming, diving,

soaring, flying

movement everywhere.

"Fly high above,

   swim deep below,

      then fill the earth and multiply

   and spread the word:

The earth's alive!"

And so concludes a full Day Five.

"Wake up! Arise! Day Six is here":

Running, leaping,

crawling, creeping

creatures everywhere.

"Beasts of every

   kind spring forth

      from grandest to the very least,

both wild and tame.

Now all's in place:

It's time to form the human race."

"I've saved the best part for the last":

Living, breathing,

thinking, dreaming

people everywhere.

"My image shall

reflect in you,

for through your life I sanctify

all that I've made.

I've done this much

Because you are my crowning touch."

"One favor I shall ask of you:

Guard, protect,

adore, respect

and keep my world in peace.

Care for this earth,

watch over life,

make sure that all are treated fair."

Day Six is through

And makes God smile;

"I think I'll rest a little while."

The Seventh Day completes the week:

Rest, refresh

spirit and flesh,

for God has blessed this day.

"These words of mine

have made a world:

with all I see, I am well pleased!

Now time begins,

But I'm not done:

My work on earth has just begun."